IMAGES

Sutton

Christmas Show Week, 1907. Haddon Road, on the left, is now only an alleyway into Tesco's multi-storey car park since the one way traffic system was built through the road. On the right of the picture is The Three Cups coffee house, a well known local landmark at the time.

IMAGES OF ENGLAND

Sutton

Jane E.M. Jones

NONSUCH

Above: The cricket team of Sutton County School, Throwley Road, *c.* 1920.

Front cover: Children watching the raising of the Union Jack at All Saints School, Benhilton on Empire day, *c.* 1910.

First published 1998
This new pocket edition 2006
Images unchanged from first edition

Nonsuch Publishing Limited
The Mill, Brimscombe Port,
Stroud, Gloucestershire, GL5 2QG
www.nonsuch-publishing.com

Nonsuch Publishing is an imprint of Tempus Publishing Group

British Library Cataloguing in Publication Data.
A catalogue record for this book is available from the British Library.

ISBN 1-84588-324-1

Typesetting and origination by Nonsuch Publishing Limited
Printed in Great Britain by Oaklands Book Services Limited

Contents

Sutton Green, c. 1915

Bibliography

Five Centuries of Artists in Sutton, by Maureen Beasley.
Sutton in Old Photographs, by Patricia Berry.
All Our Yesterdays, by Ian Bradley, June Broughton and Douglas Cluett.
The Past in Pictures, by June Broughton.
Sutton, A Pictorial History, by Frank Burgess.
Cheam, Belmont and Worcester Park, by Frank Burgess.
100 Years of Public Health in Sutton, by Lyn Charlesworth, Derek Eves, Ron Michell, Chris Reid.
The Story of Belmont Hospital 1853-1959, by Gareth Edwards.
A Small School in the Great War, by A.E. Jones.
Carshalton House, by A.E. Jones.
Clapham Lodge and the Bawtree Family, by Anne Knee.
A Brief History of Brambleacres and Bawtree House, by Joyce Roseberg.
Church's Directory of Sutton.
Pile's Directory of Sutton and District.
Sutton and Cheam Advertiser.

Introduction

My initial interest in the recent history of Sutton was started almost accidentally. When I first came to live in the town some years ago, like so many people I tended to think of it as part of the suburban spread of Greater London, with no real discernible thread of continuous history as a town with its own identity, in its businesses, its buildings or most of all its families. How very mistaken that view was.

I acquired by chance an old postcard of the road where I was living and although with the spread of modern building it was easy to believe that almost nothing featured on the old picture was still with us, closer examination showed how easy it was to identify today exact spots from the scene of almost a hundred years ago. A wall here, a pair of fine gate posts there. An ornate chimney peeping over the roofs and a young tree which today is a grand specimen. Other postcards followed, building a fuller picture of Sutton now gone, and yet everywhere it was possible to find so many traces of those old times that were still with us.

One clue led to another and so the story continued. Where was the location of those imposing houses? Who were the families who lived in them? Are the names of roads or developments today based on the names of these prominent families? It is surely not coincidence, as their influence was far-reaching. So many questions followed, each being answered in part by more pictures and information and frequently by fortunate coincidence. Was that name or those names glimpsed in passing on the War Memorial or in the local graveyard related to the person mentioned in various Sutton records and journals? Or was it the same person? What was it about Sutton then that enabled a Charity Fête to raise money for the local hospital and attract an attendance of more than 20,000 people – a crowd which would be envied by many leading football clubs today? As I searched for pictures for this collection and the facts to describe them, the interweaving of so many people and events constantly showed Sutton to be a prosperous town with its own clear identity and civic pride.

This book can only scratch at the surface, and if it stimulates memories in some and curiosity about Sutton in many others, I hope it will give as much pleasure as a starting point as it has given to me in its compilation.

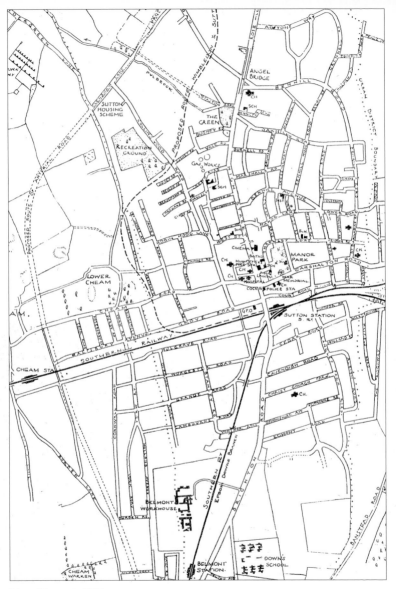

Map of Sutton in 1923

One

The High Street

Christmas Show Week, 1909.

The First Sutton railway station. The first railway to Sutton was opened in 1847. It took two years to build and cost the lives of four young men, aged between fourteen and twenty-four, who were killed in accidents during its construction and are buried in St Nicholas' churchyard. This small wooden hut served Sutton's residents as a station for nearly twenty years and if it seems very small, one must remember that Sutton had only 1,500 residents at the time.

The railway station, c. 1918. In 1865 the Epsom Downs line was opened and many additional passengers travelled on the railway as a result. In Derby week 1865, 70,000 people travelled on the new line. The old wooden shed was dismantled and moved to Sutton cricket ground on the corner of Gander Green Lane for use as a scorers' shed where it still stands today. A new station with a booking office, waiting rooms and a shop was erected. This continued in use until 1883 when it was demolished and the one shown here was opened.

The railway station, c. 1935. The population of Sutton continued to grow in the years around the end of the nineteenth and the beginning of the twentieth centuries, and with this the numbers of rail commuters increased. The new station pictured here opened in 1928 to keep pace with this growth. New motor cabs have also replaced the horse-drawn cabs outside the old station.

The Station Hotel, c. 1930. It was built in the 1870s and by the time this photograph was taken, Mr. W.A. Budd, the proprietor, was advertising music every night in the lounge pictured here. The Station Hotel has had several name changes over the years and is currently The Litten Tree.

Above: The High Street looking from the station down the hill, *c.* 1905. To the rear of the shops on the right there still stands a long length of the boundary wall of Sutton Court Estate. The wall is made up of chalk blocks, bricks and flints and is of a type probably dating back to when the house was built in the seventeenth century. At the station end are the remains of a gardener's cottage built into the wall.

Below: The Royal Library, High Street, 1905. As well as lending books on subscription to local residents, this shop also produced this postcard among many others. Postcards were bought and sold in their thousands during the Edwardian period. They were often collected in albums, and thank-you messages, arrangements for meetings and young people's gossip were sent backwards and forwards in the equivalent of our telephone conversations. One young lady in 1905 writes to her friend telling of her return journey from Croydon on an open topped, horse-drawn bus. 'Hope you got back before the rain came on. I got nearly drowned on top all the way, someone in front and behind with their umbrellas dripping on me!'

Above and below: The Cock Hotel, 1895. The first landlord recorded at this old Cock Hotel was John Killick, who died in 1639. The inn is mentioned by most writers in the coaching days and was a famous posting house which would have made a profitable trade in the days of the London to Brighton stagecoach, before the opening of the railway. It was normal at that time for more than twenty coaches to pass up and down the High Street in a day. As seen from the photograph below, Derby Day was particularly busy with passing coaches and most of Sutton's residents turned out to watch the comings and goings. The Cock had a large dance hall over the stables, which was known as Queen Anne's Room and here all the young and influential people of society would have met. During the cold winter months of the 1890s one hundred local poor children were generously invited to dinner in the Queen Anne's Room. Each was given a penny and a bag of sweets after the meal. After the new Cock Hotel was built in 1896 this old one was demolished.

The Cock Hotel, 1905. In a postcard sent to Daisy, who lived with her family in the gasworks, while she was visiting friends in Wiltshire, a friend writes: 'We shall be thinking of you on Sunday morning. I thought you would like a picture of our parting place.' We will never know what Daisy was doing on Sunday morning but know that she must have started her journey on a horse-drawn bus which between 1903 and 1905 picked up passengers outside the Cock Hotel.

The Cock Hotel, c. 1935, thirty years later than the picture above. The Cock sign has now been moved from outside the hotel to its position at the crossroads. Traffic signs attached to the ornate ironwork have also replaced the gaslights. The sign of the cockerel should possibly have been a horse as the hotel would have originally been named after a trace or 'cock horse' used to assist vehicles up the hill – hence the nursery rhyme 'Ride a cock horse'. One was used in the High Street until about 1885.

High Street, *c.* 1900. This stretch was known as Cock Hill until the 1880s. The shops on the east side, towards Carshalton, were built in 1880, ten years later than those on the west side. Before their development, the High Street was a picturesque sight, lined on the west by the chestnuts, limes and evergreens of Hill House. However, a rather unsightly chalk pit with a brick and flint cottage stood where the Municipal Offices were built on the corner of Throwley Road in 1901.

High Street, looking down the old Cock Hill in around 1938, nearly forty years later than the photograph above. The view is similar, but the shop fronts have been modernized, the Baptist church has been replaced by Ernest Shinner's new store and sadly the trees further down the High Street have disappeared. Electric traffic lights, erected two years earlier, now stand to cope with the increase of traffic.

Left: London and Provincial Bank, 1880. Designed by local architect Herbert Appleton, this was the first bank in Sutton and was described at the time as a 'visible sign of Sutton's progress'. The building still stands today, on the corner of the Town Square, and is known as 'Scruffy Murphy's'!

Below: Shinner's department store, *c.* 1938. In 1899 Ernest Shinner opened his first shop at 79 High Street. He gradually extended into all the shops in the terrace but one. By 1934 the terrace had been clad with a new shop front and in that year Ernest Shinner purchased the Baptist church and Shinner's was extended up to the corner of Hill Road. The gentleman with the sandwich board is advertising Shinner's bargains.

Opposite below: High Street and Surrey County Cinema, *c.* 1938. This cinema was built in 1921 and subsequently became The Gaumont until it was demolished in 1959. It stood where the top entrance to Times Square is situated today.

16

Above: Sutton Arcade was built by Mr Ernest Shinner in 1926. When this photograph was taken (1930) by Athelstone Bawtree one of his photographic shops was situated in the arcade. Among others were Dewey's music store and The Arcade Doggie Shop. It is to Sutton's great loss that more effort was not made to preserve and restore this lovely piece of 1920s architecture; it was demolished and a Virgin Megastore built on its site. Only two shops remain at the Throwley Way end.

High Street, Sutton, Surrey.

Above: High Street during Christmas Show Week, 1909. Trade looks brisk, with the High Street crowded in the week running up to Christmas. The Paragon confectioners is the shop whose front is in line with the fence on the right, advertising Christmas novelties. The shop was a well-known local landmark until it was demolished in 1960 so the footpath could be widened. It was rebuilt in line with its neighbours and the premises survive between Adams children's shop and the Halifax bank.

Above: High Street, 1904. These three very smartly turned-out boys are playing with hoops, which were very much a game of the time. The pillar-box on the right, erected in 1882, now stands on the corner of Manor Lane, since the High Street was pedestrianized. It is unusual in that it has no royal crest on it.

Below: Fraser's ironmongery store opened in April 1931 with a blaze of publicity. It was, however, quite a short-lived business venture as by 1934 John Perring's furniture store occupied this building on the corner of West Street. On the opposite corner Amos Odd and Sons ran their cricket bat, sports and toy shop, selling cricket bats made in the family workshop in West Street which continued in business until the 1970s.

Opposite below: High Street, 1955. There is little change to the buildings in this scene from that above from nearly half a century before; they have simply been updated. This shows how lucky the High Street was in escaping relatively unscathed during the Second World War, despite heavy bombing in Sutton. There was an incident in September 1940, when a bomb dropped on the roof of one of two public air-raid shelters behind the Greyhound Hotel. Although a hole was made in the roof, it did not come through and only two people inside were slightly injured.

High Street, c. 1935: a slightly later view, after British Home Stores was opened in 1934, but before the removal in 1938 of the beam across the road which carried the sign for the Greyhound Hotel. John Perring's furniture and bedding store had opened at the corner of West Street in the previous year.

High Street and Greyhound Hotel, 1908. This was a well-known old posting house and many day-trippers on their way to Box Hill or Epsom would stop here for refreshment. The hotel was completely rebuilt in 1873 when there was a grand opening dinner attended by many notable local people. The Greyhound was demolished in 1959 and Superdrug now stands on the site.

Hoare and Son, grocers and tea dealers, 1893. The business was established in the High Street in 1764, the business being passed down from father to son for several generations. In the middle of the nineteenth century James and Hannah Hoare ran the shop and lived here with their four daughters and son, William, who inherited the business on his father's death in 1864. This building was demolished in 1893 and the shop continued to trade as Hoare and Kilby grocers in a new shop on the site, where Vision Express is situated today, until 1902.

High Street, c. 1910. The tree shown here outside the Greyhound Hotel was eventually the last tree standing in the High Street. In 1959, when the Greyhound was demolished and a new Woolworth's store replaced it, Viola Bawtree remembered touching it with trepidation on her weekly visits to the town, not daring to believe this tree brushing the upstairs windows would be allowed to remain. Viola would have been relieved to know it did survive, until sadly destroyed in the hurricane of 1987.

High Street, 1917. This early Barclays Bank stood on the corner of Manor Place. On the right W. Walker, confectioner and manufacturer of pure sweets, sold among other things Sutton rock. Next door Mr W.F. Jaggs ran the Shaftesbury coffee and dining rooms, which offered bed and breakfast accommodation; they advertised their beds as 'well aired'.

High Street, c. 1900. Manor Parade on the right had been recently built. Grand Parade, on the other side of Manor Lane, with the new Barclays Bank on the corner (see above) was not built until 1909. The trees of Oakly Lodge can still be seen. On the left, the turning into George Street is opposite Manor Lane and Blackwater Road, the junction slightly further down. The St Nicholas Centre stands on the site of both these roads today.

The International Tea Company stores in 1905 with manager Mr C.J. Death and his staff standing outside. The store stood in Manor Parade, which is the terrace of shops where McDonalds stands today. Once, the Manor House wall stood along this stretch with the trees from the extensive gardens overhanging the High Street. The Manor House was demolished in 1895 and the area was developed in the late 1890s.

High Street, looking southwards up the hill from the corner of Benhill Street, 1912. The Grapes Hotel, built in the 1870s, offered among other things 'superior foreign wines and spirits and billiards, pool and pyramids'. It was a well known landmark destination for trams, which terminated here for many years. Although the pub has had several name changes and is presently a sports bar, it is still known as the Grapes on bus timetables.

Above: The corner of Benhill Street, showing Stevens' the butcher's shop, during Christmas Show Week in 1908. The shop is presently empty since the post office has moved to the St Nicholas Centre. The old bicycle shed still standing at the rear has a wall made of chalk blocks which would have been the wall of Stevens' slaughterhouse, but as these chalk block walls have not been used in Sutton since about 1700 it must be a remnant of a much earlier farm building belonging to Benhill Farm which was situated on this site. Benhill Farm was adjacent to Benhill Wood; it covered much of the land around where Benhill Avenue runs today and was the largest farm in Sutton. William Wilson lived with his wife Jane in the farmhouse, which stood where the shops at the corner of Benhill Avenue and Throwley Way stand today. After Jane's death in 1842 William moved to his second residence in Blackfriars and most of the land of Benhill Farm was sold, leading to much of the development on this side of the High Street. William and Jane are buried in St Nicholas' churchyard with three of their children, including two who died in young adulthood.

Opposite below: High Street in around 1903, showing the old Red Lion Inn before it was rebuilt in 1907. This old inn is referred to as far back as 1799. The far two shops on the left, Clarke and Son's grocers and L.G. Gower's corn merchants, have been demolished to allow for the widening of Marshall's Road, now part of the one way traffic system. However, Stock and Wallis' stationer and bookseller, now The Bengal Tandoori, remains standing on its own, contrasting with all the development around it.

Above: The High Street at the junction of Greenford Road in 1910. In 1745, milestones were introduced from Westminster and London Bridge to Banstead Downs with more added in 1755 to reach Reigate and through Cheam to Ewell. The one in this photograph still stands today, as do those on the road to Rosehill Roundabout, on Brighton Road nearly opposite the end of Christchurch Park and on Cheam Road near the end of York Road.

High Street Sutton. Xmas Show Week, 1908.

S&W.Series.3.

Looking towards the Crown public house during Christmas Show Week in 1908, from a series of thirteen postcards produced by Stock and Wallis' stationers (see previous page) in that year. These sold in their thousands during Christmas Show Week, for 1d each. In October a meeting was held at the Public Hall for the local traders to discuss the celebrations. The shops were responsible for the decorations in the High Street adjacent to them and a total cost was agreed of £128 10s. Sadly though, Christmas was marred by an event which shocked the local community. A man who had moved from Camberwell and leased 72 High Street (where Virgin Megastore stands today) for use as a tea rooms and confectioner's shop, became increasingly depressed about the lack of success of his business. A few weeks before Christmas, PC Davies, after breaking into the premises early one morning, found that the man had murdered his wife and then killed himself. This terrible double tragedy was widely reported as having upset local people very much, and the constant rain after all the hard work decorating the town led to Christmas 1908 being one of the least happy in Sutton's history.

Two

Churches

St Nicholas' church, *c.* 1915.

St. Nicholas Parish Church, Sutton

Parish Church, Sutton

Above: St Nicholas' church (pictured here *c.* 1910) was first mentioned in the Domesday Book of 1086. The present building was rebuilt in 1864 to accommodate Sutton's growing population. The plain glass in the windows on the north side of the church replaces the stained glass blown out by a large bomb on the night of 24 September 1940. Although the bomb left a crater 26ft across and 20ft deep and several graves and tombstones simply vanished, the church was not seriously damaged and services continued throughout the war.

Left: St Nicholas' churchyard in 1920. Many of Sutton's notable residents are buried here, including Mr George Orme, the last owner of the Manor House, who was buried here with his first wife and three infant children in 1895. On the day of his funeral there was a violent thunderstorm and the four black stallions pulling the hearse took fright and overturned the coffin. Workers from the Manor Estate then had to carry the coffin to the churchyard in the storm. Also buried here are the 185 orphans from the Metropolitan District School whose graves are marked by a small memorial erected by St Nicholas' church Sunday school children in 1921.

Above and below: The interior of St Nicholas' church, 1905. The Revd Herbert William Turner MA was rector of St Nicholas' church from July 1886 until his death in 1922, after ten years as Minister of Christchurch. He was immensely popular, described as a man with such magnetism that he drew men and women around him; his original sermons were always delivered to packed congregations. He was involved in much local charity work, such as setting up a committee of local tradesmen to provide dinners at the Shaftesbury coffee rooms during cold winter months for 2,500 local poor children in batches of 150. Here the rector and his committee served them roast beef, vegetables and plum pudding. Revd Turner lived with his wife, Ellen, and nine children at The Rectory in West Street (below). Ellen died after a long illness in 1897 and in 1899 the Revd Turner married Miss Harriet Leete of Eversley, Grange Road. His beloved daughter Evelyn also died of diphtheria here in 1895 aged nineteen. There is a memorial window dedicated to her in St Nicholas' church, illustrating the life of St Faith.

No. 3. Benhilton Church, Sutton

All Saints' church, Benhilton, *c.* 1920. In the 1860s a committee was formed to discuss the building of a new church in Sutton. Samuel Teulon, a respected church designer, was the architect and meetings were held to discuss plans at Southfields, Sutton Common Road, home of Anthony Locke, a local merchant and builder. In 1865 Benhilton church was built. Samuel Teulon died before the church was completed and coincidentally it was Anthony Locke's son Edward, now an architect, who as a boy had been present at the early planning, who completed the north side of the church.

VIEW FROM BENHILTON CHURCH, SUTTON.   Photo: Blacker.

All Saints' churchyard, *c.* 1925. The new church built high on a hill dominated north Sutton, the church bells chiming the evening hymn at 5 p.m. every day. In 1944 bombs destroyed the original east window, damaged the Vicarage and school and completely destroyed the parish hall. The stained glass windows were finally replaced in 1964 but sadly further restoration work had to be carried out in 1986 after the church roof was struck by lightning.

A Sunday school outing, 6 June 1931. Everyone from All Saints' church Sunday school who attended enjoyed this outing to Littlehampton. However, on the same day the Congregational church took a group of Sunday school children to Bognor and there was a very worrying time when a young lad went missing. Eventually he was found wandering the streets with an empty ginger beer bottle trying to find the shop from where it was bought to recover the penny on its return!

A wedding group at All Saints' church, Benhilton, c. 1960. For over 130 years Sutton's residents have passed through these church doors which will have seen so many happy and sad events. Pictured here is one of the hundreds of happy couples who have celebrated their wedding day in this church.

Wesleyan Church, Sutton.

The Wesleyan Methodist church, Carshalton Road, 1906. Built in 1884, this replaced a smaller chapel in Clifton Crescent, Benhill Street, that opened in 1867. After the Methodists built their present church in 1907, on the corner of St Nicholas Road and Cheam Road, the building became an electric theatre called the Sutton Hippodrome, then an engineering works until the 1950s. A few months after this picture was taken the small wooden schoolroom to the right of the church was unfortunately destroyed by fire (see below).

Fire at the Wesleyan church school, Carshalton Road, 1 September 1906. The fire brigade was called to the school adjoining the church late one Saturday night. The fire had already taken hold and the wooden school was doomed from the start, but the fire brigade managed to save the church and the stable next door even though both suffered fire and water damage.

Right: The new Wesleyan church, Cheam Road, in 1907 with the hoardings still in place prior to its opening in 1908. The card is from a collection of chatty postcards sent from friends who lived locally to Daisy Carpenter who lived with her family at Sutton gasworks, where her father Stephen was engineer; the message merely says, 'Hope you have left your nerves behind. Are you ready to go up this tower?'

Below: The Wesleyan church schoolrooms, 1908. The church opened in this year replaced the smaller Church in Carshalton Road. It was built in fifteenth-century Gothic style and could accommodate about 580 worshippers. The frontage in Hill Road was occupied by these schoolrooms. With the church parlours above the schoolrooms, they formed one of the most complete blocks of church buildings in Surrey at the time.

Above: The Congregational church in 1909, showing clearly the position where it used to stand, next to the police station. Built in 1889 on land donated by the Sutton Court Estate, it replaced a smaller chapel in Benhill Street. Sutton Court was the home of three generations of the influential Ruck family in the nineteenth century.

Below: The interior of the Congregational church, 1900. It originally had a stained-glass rose window above the altar. As the church faced south, it had to be removed as the congregation complained of the sun shining in their eyes during services.

Opposite below: The Baptist church, 1908. It was opened in 1873 on the corner of Hill Road and the High Street to a design by local architect Herbert Appleton, who was only twenty years old at the time. It was the only church in the High Street and must have been quite noisy with returning day-trippers passing through the town on a Sunday evening. In 1934 the present Baptist church was opened in Cheam Road and this building was demolished to make way for an extension to the Shinner's store.

Above: A Congregational church group, 1900. Pictured here are Alfred and Matilda Bawtree, seated second and third from the left on the front row, and their eldest son Alfred, standing third from the left on the back row. The gentleman with the beard standing on the left was Mr Myers, Sunday school teacher. Alfred and Matilda's youngest son, Ivan, who was six at the time, remembered being so frightened of his appearance he hid under the schoolroom table refusing to come out.

United Methodist Free church, Marshall's Road, *c.* 1910. It was also opened in 1873, succeeding a smaller building in West Street. Capable of accommodating 200 people, it cost £550 to build. A new schoolroom was added and opened on 31 August 1879. The one way traffic system today where Marshall's Road leads into Throwley Way makes a very different picture than this quiet residential road.

Christchurch, *c.* 1900. In March 1876 a temporary iron building was built in Brighton Road, near Cavendish Road, for use as a place of worship for the people of the highly populated south Sutton area with Revd Herbert Turner as rector. Twelve years later the track between Langley Park Road and Brighton Road became Christchurch Park and the new church was opened.

St Barnabas' church, c. 1900. In 1880 the needs of the residents of Sutton's Newtown area for a place of worship were recognized. Until then services were held in a small room in Lind Road. Unfortunately the plot of land secured caused problems with the foundations and the church had to be built below street level, taking much longer and costing much more than originally expected.

St Barnabas' church interior, 1934. The Revd C.J. Boden came as vicar from Wimbledon parish church and the church was consecrated in 1884. There was a schoolroom at the west end of the church with space for about 250 children and it was overlooked by the Vicarage from a site across allotments on the far side of Lower Road, where a block of flats called Maple Court stands today.

Our Lady of the Rosary Catholic church, St Barnabas Road, 1904. The Bishop of Southwark sent Father Daniel Ferris as the first priest in charge of the new church then called St Mary's, which opened for Sutton's Catholics in 1882. Father Ferris began a school in a little iron building near the church in 1890.

Our Lady of the Rosary Catholic church interior, 1904. Shortly after the school started, the building was condemned and part of the church was used as a school during the week and reverted to a church on Sundays. This situation was not ideal and the Daughters of the Cross came to the rescue, allowing a school to be built in the grounds of Carshalton House, which opened in 1894.

Three

West Sutton:
Towards Cheam

Cheam Road Junction, *c.* 1911.

Cheam Road, Sutton.

Above: Cheam Road Cinema (seen here in 1913) was built in 1911 and replaced three 'electric theatres' – the Bio Picture Hall, held in the basement of a shop on the corner of Sutton Arcade, another behind where Clarks stands today and The Hippodrome in Carshalton Road. In 1953 it became The Curzon until it was completely rebuilt in 1971 and became Studio 1,2,3 then Cannon Cinema. It was closed in 1992 and at present Legends night club occupies the building.

Opposite above: Cheam Road with the Cock Hotel in the distance, *c.* 1910. This was the main road between Croydon and Guildford and there would have been a flow of traffic between the old towns along the route. Before 1848 the Cheam Road tollgate would have been situated on this stretch, but it had to be moved to avoid losses caused by new roads such as Grove Road forming a bypass. The tollgate finally ended up on the corner of Gander Green Lane until its removal in 1881.

Opposite below: Cheam Road, 1926. This peaceful view towards Trinity church shows how many trees once stood in this road, creating an almost rural atmosphere. Very few of these trees have survived today. After its closure in 1961, the buildings of Sutton High School for Boys, on the left, were used for various business purposes until they were demolished to allow for the building of Safeway, which stands on the site today .

Cheam Road, 1907. The house on the left, Friargate, still stands today. Robert and Elizabeth Overton who lived here with their eight children were a typical large Victorian family, but coming from the middle classes they could afford a housemaid, a cook and a children's nurse to look after them and their large house. Today the house is divided into flats.

Cheam Road, 1905. These attractive villas still form a similar picture on the road into Sutton. On the left the overgrown chalk pit, where Sutton cricket ground stands today, was a favourite place in the nineteenth century for tramps to eat and sleep en route through Surrey from one workhouse to another, despite a sign on the gate saying 'Beware: man traps are set'.

The post office, Grove Road, 1909. Opened in 1907, this replaced a much smaller post office in the High Street. At the time this photograph was taken there were ten collections a day from most of Sutton's fifty-two post boxes. The earliest was at 6am and the latest at 10pm from the post box in the High Street. Sutton's houses and businesses had four deliveries of letters and parcels daily except on Sundays when there was no parcel delivery.

Grove Road, c. 1910. Grove Avenue, running from this road to Cheam Road, was developed on the site of Sutton Hall, the only house in the area during the beginning of the nineteenth century. In 1872 John Wanklyn, a merchant, bought the hall, vacating his home in Sandy Lane, Cheam, for his daughter Maggie and new husband Egerton Ruck. The marriage was celebrated as a great union of two respected local families who had been friends for many years. But in less than four years tragedy had struck as John died suddenly aged forty-eight and Maggie died aged twenty-three, leaving Egerton a widower with two small children.

Church Road in 1917. This now forms part of the one-way traffic system and is called St. Nicholas Way. One of the two houses which stood on the corner where the civic offices and the central library stand today was Stafford House, home for many years of Dendy Napper and his family, who owned the Steam Mills in the High Street situated behind his baker's shop, which stood where Adams children's shop is today. Dendy, a resident of Sutton for fifty years, held many public offices including churchwarden of St Nicholas' church.

Sutton Hospital, c. 1920. Its position is shown clearly here in Hill Road, with the ambulance parked outside, to the back of the Wesleyan church. It was built in 1902 on land given by Sir Ralph Forster of The Grange, Mulgrave Road, and replaced the cottage hospital in Bushey Road. Before ambulances were used, handcarts on which accident cases were moved to the hospital were housed in a nearby shed. The Moon on the Hill public house stands on the site today.

Hill Road c. 1905. The Public Hall on the left opened in 1879 as a central meeting place for the growing town of Sutton. The house next to the Public Hall behind the fence is Acacia Villa, home of local photographer and estate agent William Hind, who lived here with his wife Maria and nine children until his death in 1901. Mr Hind took many of the fine early photographs of Sutton published in local history books.

Sutton District Laundry Company at 10 West Street next to West Street National School, c. 1930. It featured a special 'economy service', whereby staff collected, washed, ironed and returned linen at moderate prices. These sorts of services were popular at a time before houses had washing machines.

Robin Hood Lane looking north from Cheam Road, *c.* 1915. The flint-stone wall on the left belonging to Fernwood, a house built in the mid-nineteenth century where the Holiday Inn car park is situated today, was typical of the type of wall used all over Sutton at this time. Many of these walls can still be found tucked away between modern flats and gardens of houses, remnants of much earlier homes.

Robin Hood Lane looking south towards Cheam Road, *c.* 1905. On the left beyond the houses is Court Lodge. It was the old farmhouse for an ancient farm in the area. Its boundary wall runs along the churchyard and is another old flint wall. Although part of it was destroyed by a bomb which fell in the churchyard during the Second World War, some still remains today.

The Robin Hood Hotel, West Street, c. 1900. Built in the 1870s, this was one of twenty-six licensed premises in Sutton towards the end of the last century. Before 1864 there was no piped water in Sutton and ale was a popular drink at twopence a pint. The pub was the main place for social contact among ordinary people and Sutton's residents would have drunk at one of the many little alehouses including Crosskeys in Vernon Road, Eagle Tavern in Lind Road and Victory Beerhouse in William Road, which still stands today.

Above: Strathearn Road, 1916. Apart from the absence of cars there are great similarities between this picture and the present day. This road is within the rectangle bordered by Gander Green Lane, Clensham Lane, Balaam Lane (now Collingwood Road) and Cheam Fields (now Tate Road), which was known as the Little Manor, held by Simon de Codyngton, Lord of the Manor of Cuddington in 1372.

Collingwood Road, Sutton.

Seeger's Photo Series.

Above: Collingwood Road, 1911. Until the 1880s this road was known as Balaam Lane, a corruption of the name Wynefold de Baalun, a fifteenth-century land holder who had a mill on the tenement, paying ten shillings a year rent. His name still survives in the area in Balaam House. There was also a mint distillery in Balaam Lane. Part of the sheds still exist today as a Grade II listed building on the corner of Beauchamp Road. In the autumn peppermint was distilled for oil, giving an overpowering scent in the area for a week or two. Some of the oldest cottages in Sutton are the eight in Collingwood Road at the corner of Crown Road. They appeared on a map of 1841, when agricultural workers lived here surrounded by fields. Life was hard for working-class families at the time and they were uneducated, unable even to sign their names. They had large families, nine or ten children being normal of which many died in infancy, and many had illegitimate children brought up within the large family. By their early teens the boys had become agricultural labourers like their father and the girls usually went into service. They worked hard for little pay all their lives and there was the constant threat of Epsom workhouse, which was where many of Sutton's poor old people ended their lives.

Opposite below: Sherwood Park Road, 1905. It was developed in the 1890s through Cheam Fields and most of the large villas still stand today. The sender of this postcard tells of visiting a circus in Sutton. Sanger's circus visited the town annually at around the end of the nineteenth and the beginning of the twentieth centuries, arriving with a grand procession through the High Street, bringing animals such as elephants, tigers and monkeys and causing much excitement.

49

Above: Fire in Haddon Road, Sutton. On 23 September 1923 fire broke out at Leyton timberyard in Haddon Road and spread to the houses. Within three minutes the fire pump and men were on the scene. Fences were removed in Brandon Road to stop the fire spreading in that direction. In the north-east of the yard was a blacksmith's shop adjoining a row of cottages in Chandlers Alley (where Tesco stands today); if these had been burnt there would have been great danger to the High Street.

Left: School furniture was removed from Sutton West Infants' School, shown here, and piled up in the playground away from the fire. The fire raged for several hours and only a constant deluge of water and the assistance of Carshalton fire brigade prevented it from spreading further.

Many of Haddon Road's residents were at the County Cinema in the High Street, where the orchestra was stopped and people were asked to return to their houses which were in great danger. There was great panic and people's belongings were thrown into the street. By the next morning Haddon Road was a pitiful sight, windows and even frames had been broken, furniture, crockery and ornaments were left scattered in the rain. More damage had been done in this way than by the fire itself. Although there was no loss of life there was much human tragedy. For example, Mr C. Martyn, an ex-serviceman, had worked hard after the war trying to build an umbrella-mending business in the front room of his house, but machinery and customers' goods were badly damaged. An appeal fund was started to help people who had been made temporarily homeless and had lost furniture and belongings.

Orchard Road, Sutton.

Seeger's Photo Series.

Orchard Road, which formed part of the 'little manor of Sutton', in 1910. There were originally many French tenants in this area. One John Orchart farmed the tenement known as the Beauchamp Estate. This was a farm of forty acres, where John lived in the farmhouse called Beauchamp Lodge, with his sisters Mary and Helen, from the 1850s until the late 1890s. Beauchamp Lodge was reached down a track through the fields from Collingwood Road, which ran along the line of Orchard Road. Around 1900 the land was sold off and Beauchamp Road and Orchard Road, named after John Orchart, now stand on part of the farmland. The farmhouse still survives today at the end of Beauchamp Road.

Opposite above: St James Road, 1905. This was another road with large villas with names such as Park Villa and Henley Villa, many of which have survived today. How would the young lady in the photograph, stealing a kiss from her suitor, feel if she had known how public her kiss would become so many years later?

Opposite below: York Road, 1904. Until its development in the 1870s, York Road was merely a farm track forming part of the route to the Banstead Downs from North Cheam Road. It was used for driving cattle, sheep and poultry between markets.

St. James Road, Sutton.

Above: Gander Green Lane (seen here *c.* 1920) was the western boundary of the Manor of Sutton. Large numbers of geese were driven to market down its wide, green grass verges, giving it its name. The fence behind the couple on the left belonged to Lower Cheam House, built by Phillip Antrobus around 1800. A large, luxuriously decorated house, it was home of the Antrobus family for a hundred years. On the death of Hugh Antrobus in 1899 the house was sold and in 1933 it was demolished, the land being used for a number of houses including those in Antrobus Close.

Left: Gander Green Lane, *c.* 1900. This delightfully rural view of the lane shows the fields stretching out on either side. The roadside pond on the right, with the white posts in front of it, was situated a short distance in front of where West Sutton station stands today.

Above: West Sutton station, Gander Green Lane, 1930. Opened in early 1930, this was one of the two stations in Sutton on the new Wimbledon line, with electric trains travelling via Holborn and Wimbledon to Waterloo. There has been much controversy recently about the derelict state of this station and although currently being upgraded, it seems a shame that the stations on this line have fallen into such disrepair, when they were opened with such local pride.

Below: The Lord Nelson, Stonecot Hill, 1938. The Roman Stane Street bordered the Manor of Sutton on its north-west boundary from Gander Green Lane to Morden. The name Stonecot is possibly a derivative of this. Around 1538, Henry VIII had stones transported along this road to build Nonsuch Palace. When the Epsom Downs racecourse came into operation in 1779 crowds travelled along Stane Street, stopping at The Lord Nelson Inn for refreshment.

Love Lane (here in around 1909) formed part of the ancient pathway between Sutton and Cheam churches. Running along Camden Road, Tate Road, across Gander Green Lane and down Love Lane, the route was a narrow footpath; the Tate Road stretch was a field path with farm gates at either end. There is evidence to suggest that this route between the two parishes has been in use since the sixteenth century.

Four

South Sutton:
Towards Belmont

Brighton Road at the corner of Cedar Road, c. 1910.

Sutton. *Mulgrave Road.* *The cap is a great Success.*

W. Pile Ltd , Sutton.

Mulgrave Road, 1903. Mulgrave Hall, pictured here, was one of the first houses developed in the area and still stands today. Built by Mr. E.H. Rabbits, a local builder and businessman, as his Sutton home, the grounds extended to Brighton Road. When the Downs railway line was built in 1865 the railway company built a light wooden bridge to connect either side of his estate.

An early motor car travels leisurely along a quiet Mulgrave Road, 1909. Notice the little dog enjoying the ride at the front. It must indeed have been a more leisurely pace as in 1904 a Kensington man was fined £3 for driving along the Brighton Road at 26mph despite being shouted at several times by people telling him to slow down!

Cornwall Road, 1909. Mrs Jean Birnage is standing at the door of Cornwall Lodge with her three children. Cornwall Road is unusual in that unlike most residential roads in Sutton the large houses have all remained and there has been no development of flats.

Mulgrave Road, 1931. These five new shops at the corner of the High Street and the flats above called Mulgrave Court were completed in the summer of that year. Some of the first shops to occupy the premises were P.H. Parrot Ltd, a tailor, and Sutton Dyers and Cleaners.

Above and below: Brighton Road looking towards Belmont from the junction of Cedar Road, *c.* 1905 (above). There was obviously much coming and going to the smart houses of south Sutton, where so many commuters settled after the coming of the railway in 1845. Looking towards Sutton (below), the road on the right was Worcester Gardens, which has now been obliterated by a multi-storey car park. The sender of this postcard who lived in Cumnor Road writes to a friend in Streatham Hill: 'It has turned out such a wet, stormy evening that I thought if it is wet tomorrow it would be better not to visit you. The children would not be able to get out and I am sure you would be worried to have Jackie indoors all day.' How marvellous to be able to be able to post a card at 8.45pm and be so certain it would arrive the following morning. One wonders though what was wrong with Jackie that he could not be allowed indoors!

Cedar Road, 1907. The Cedars Estate, after which this road was named, was a large house with grounds that extended from the railway to Cedar Road and Langley Park Road to the east. One of the Lebanon cedar trees from within the grounds, which gave the estate its name, still survives today, standing in the Quadrant. It is said to date back to the mid-sixteenth century when Henry VIII introduced them to the area.

Cedar Road, 1905. The large house called The Cedars was demolished around 1900. Among the local notable people who lived on the estate was the influential Annand family. Alexander Annand owned the Benhill Woods and also Greenshaw Farm, which ran from the woods to Rosehill. Sophia Annand died in 1835 and her husband Alexander in 1847. They are buried in the Annand vault inside St Nicholas' church.

Langley Park Road was originally named Goodenoughs Lane after the local Goodenough family (see p. 74). The hill above the railway bridge on this road was once known as Cat's Brain Hill, which was a phrase from Buckinghamshire indicating an outcrop of chalk and clay. The houses in this picture (from 1904) stood opposite Christchurch Park where Milestone Close is situated today.

Cavendish Road, 1910. When this road was developed in the 1870s there would have been far fewer, if any, gas lights. There were only 133 gas lights in the whole village burning from sunset to 2am. At this time there was no public lighting in Cheam or Belmont. Although Sutton had gas from 1856 many cottages still used paraffin oil lamps until 1900.

Brighton Road, 1905. The cottage pictured here at the corner of Cavendish Road belonged to Wellesley Lodge, said to be the first house to be built in Brighton Road in the early 1860s. It stood in extensive grounds where Copse Hill is situated today and was built for Montgomery Martin, a Northern Irish gentleman who worked for many years as assistant Colonial Secretary. He compiled fourteen volumes entitled *The British Colonies*.

Brighton Road in 1908, at the corner of Christchurch Park looking towards Sutton. To cope with the increase in traffic from London to Brighton, in September 1815 a strip of land was purchased on the west side of the lane, the side towards Cheam, and the bank was cut away to allow for widening. The east side still has the original bank which is why the houses on this side are above road level and the houses on the west side are below it. The imposing gates on the left of this photograph belonged to Haselmere (see p. 65).

Christchurch Park in c. 1910. This road was developed in the 1880s from a track which ran from Langley Park Road to Brighton Road, after the building of Christchurch. The beautiful copper beech trees, so much a part of this road, were under threat of destruction in August 1958. The Sutton and Cheam Society was formed to save them. This society also played a part in the preservation of the old cottages at Cheam.

Egmont Road, c. 1905. Developed in the 1880s, this road was named after Lord Egmont, a prominent local resident at the time, who lived at Nork House, Banstead, and was president of Sutton district fire brigade.

Haselmere, Brighton Road, in 1918. This house was designed by local architect Herbert Appleton for his brother William in the 1880s. William Appleton, a tea merchant like his father, lived here with his wife Bessie, sons Bernard and Harold, daughters Florence and Dora and a cook, housemaid and nurse. Harold died in young adulthood and after Bessie's death in 1928 William lived in the house with his eldest daughter Florence until his death in 1940. The house was demolished in the 1960s and a block of flats called Dunsfold Court stands on the site today. The original nameplate remains on the wall outside and a magnificent cedar tree still stands in the grounds that the Appleton children would have played in over a hundred years ago.

Worcester Road, c. 1905. Comfortably-off Victorian families, typically with many children and two or three domestic servants, lived in the large houses here which were developed in the 1870s. One such family was the Bawtrees who moved into their house Brambleacres in 1871. The builder of the house, a man called Overton, suggested that the then new approach road should be called Bawtree Road. However, Samuel Bawtree felt that this was improper and so the road was named Overton Road after the builder.

The Grange, c. 1930. The Grange stood in extensive grounds South of Mulgrave Road. Although the house has been demolished, three attractive lodges still remain. One next to the pavement in Mulgrave Road was originally the coachman's cottage which stood in front of extensive stables. One prominent resident was Sir Ralph Forster, High Sheriff of Surrey, who was the first and last baronet, his only son dying in 1915 from wounds sustained in the First World War.

Grange Road, c. 1905. Only a couple of the large houses built for Sutton's professional people in the 1870s stand today, although many house names have survived. One, Ormesby, was home of a local solicitor named Algernon Crook, chairman of Sutton District Council. His son, Leslie, a Captain in the Queen's West Surrey Regiment, was awarded the Military Cross for gallantry during the Battle of the Somme in the First World War. He sadly went on to be killed, aged 26, at the third Battle of Ypres in 1917. A block of flats called Ormesby stands on the site of the house today.

Above: Sutton and Cheam Carnival. On 11 July 1931, after months of preparation, a carnival and fête to raise money for the building of the Sutton and Cheam Hospital was attended by 22,000 people in Collingwood Road Recreation Ground. It was in bright sunshine that a procession of decorated cars set off from North Cheam, wound through back roads around Cheam and Sutton, until its final stretch down the High Street and Bushey Road to the Recreation Ground. The float above shows Beauty Queen Miss Pat Louis accompanied by her child attendants.

Right: Ron and Ernest Webb were among the hundreds of people collecting money throughout the day. Local banks worked voluntarily late into the night counting close to a ton of coins. The fête continued until midnight with attractions such as steam roundabouts, Punch and Judy, pony rides and swing boats. With the Sutton Red Cross Band providing the music for dancing in the evening, this enormously popular day raised £2,140 towards the building of the new Sutton and Cheam Hospital (see p. 68).

Sutton and Cheam Hospital, Brighton Road, 1931. Opened on 30 September 1931, this hospital was entirely funded by public donations at a cost of £50,000, including £5,000 raised by the Sutton and Cheam Traders' Association to pay for a Traders' Ward. It replaced the smaller hospital in Hill Road and consisted of twenty-two men's beds, twenty-two women's beds, twelve beds for private patients and twelve children's cots. It also had modern outpatient, massage, radiant heat and x-ray departments.

The Station, Belmont.

Belmont station, c. 1916. Cobbett wrote in Rural Rides in 1823: 'The road from London to Reigate through Sutton is about as villainous a tract as England contains.' Indeed, in the very early part of the nineteenth century this area and its one beer shop called Gibbons House had a notorious reputation. It is said that John Gibbons made his fortune in the California gold rush, returning to the area and building the California public house around 1860. This station was originally called California after the pub. It was later changed to Belmont after which the village was named.

Five

East Sutton:
Towards Carshalton

Manor Park Gates from Throwley Road, *c.* 1920.

The police station, Carshalton Road, 1909. Opened shortly before this picture was taken, the new police station contained a magistrates' courthouse. One of the first cases heard there was of four young Sutton men, all from very good homes, arrested by PC Davies after midnight for throwing snowballs in Brighton Road despite being warned that they would break a light. The case was dropped after the bench decided that although they had been rather rowdy, they had only been having a little fun.

Manor Park in 1914 consisted of about three acres and was designed more as a public garden than a recreation ground. Although a strip of the park was lost when Throwley Way was developed, the park still remains a picturesque feature so close to the town centre. Still remaining is the ornamental fountain presented by Mr Charles Yates in 1931.

Manor Park, c. 1915. As well as being a place for local children to come and play, the portable stage shown here was used by amateur repertory companies presenting plays and local military bands would perform concerts on Sundays. On summer evenings dancing attracted both young and old and in the 1930s a physical training instructor took an early keep-fit class.

SUTTON THE PARK, & WAR MEMORIAL.   57312

Manor Park House, c. 1924. Built in 1871 for John Ruck of Sutton Court, the house remained in the family until Maria Ruck's death in 1894. From around the end of the nineteenth and the beginning of the twentieth centuries it was Sutton Preparatory School, until the First World War when it was used to house Belgian refugees. From 1920 until 1928 boys from Sutton County School were taught here when the school in Throwley Road became overcrowded. The house is best remembered for its use as Sutton Central Library for many years until its demolition in 1976.

John Ruck, c. 1850. Born in 1811 in London, John, a wine merchant, married Maria Sayer and moved to Sutton Court, Carshalton Road, in 1847. One of the largest and oldest estates in the village, the house stood where the police station stands today, with grounds extending southwards to the railway lines and eastwards to the chalk pit where B & Q is situated today. The gardens were beautifully tended as John was vice-president of the Sutton and Cheam Horticultural Society and the annual show was held in alternate years at Sutton Court and Lower Cheam house, home of Hugh Antrobus. They were great social events with brass bands in attendance.

Maria Ruck, c. 1850. John and Maria moved into Manor Park House in 1871 with their six children, Charles, Frederick, Ellen, Egerton, Harriet and Gordon, and had several servants including a butler, a cook a ladies' maid and housemaids. John died in 1888, followed by Maria on Christmas Day 1894, after which the house was sold and Ellen, Harriet and Gordon moved to Eversley, Langley Park Road, which still stands. The family supported many local charitable causes. Harriet, unusually for a woman at the time, held the respected position of Guardian of the North East Ward of Sutton, meaning that she was one of the six residents of Sutton managing the workhouse and dealing with applications for poor relief.

Charles Ruck, c. 1865. The eldest son of John and Maria was a wine merchant like his father and youngest brother, Gordon. He married Florence Turner from Benhilton, Sutton and moved to Reigate, having four sons, Sydney, George, Cecil and Vincent. Egerton, a director of Sutton Water Company, remained locally and lived in Sandy Lane, Cheam where he brought up two children on his own after his wife Maggie died young. They were a family who had many friends as well as being greatly respected by the local working-class people; the community was shocked when in 1905 Gordon and Egerton both died suddenly from heart attacks, within five weeks of each other. Egerton is buried in St Dunstan's churchyard in Cheam and Gordon is buried with John and Maria in St Nicholas' churchyard.

Carshalton Road, 1918. With Robert Hogg the butcher's shop on the left and The Elms, an early Victorian house used as the waterworks offices by the time this picture was taken, on the right, there are great similarities between this picture and the present day. The turning on the left at the top of the hill is Langley Park Road, which was known as Goodenoughs Lane until the 1870s. It was named after a local landowner, William Goodenough, who lived with his wife Ann and three daughters Maria, Elizabeth and Sarah at Goodenoughs Pit until the 1840s. This was the old chalk pit where B & Q stands today.

Opposite above: Carshalton Road, 1905. From the corner of Sutton Grove looking towards Sutton, the house on the left which was called Shawlands still stands and is an old people's residential home called Sandilands Lodge. A young man called Will sent this postcard to his friend Carrie saying: 'This is the road I have to walk along to go home from work, it is a very pretty road.' Will would certainly be surprised by the constant stream of traffic today.

Opposite below: Wentworth, Carshalton Road, 1914. Home of the Bennett family, this was one of the large houses along this road which have nearly all been demolished. Modern terraced houses and flats predominate today and on the site where Wentworth stood are now numbers 240-254 Carshalton Road.

Sutton. Carshalton Road.

Lind Road, built as the main road of Sutton New Town in the 1860s, seen here *c.* 1900. Flintstones from St Nicholas' church, which was demolished in 1864, were used to build walls and cottages. One of these walls can still be seen, recently restored, on the right hand corner opposite the Jenny Lind public house. The shop in the photograph is W. Lockett, a grocer here for many years.

Carshalton Grove, running from Carshalton Road to Westmead Road, 1905. The houses had names such as Laurel and Holly Villas and most of them still stand today. In the distance can be seen the fields of Shorts Farm which occupied the land north of Westmead Road. The farmhouse was situated at Westmead Corner, at the end of the present-day Shorts Road. After the First World War the land was sold and new roads were laid out, all named after English poets, now known locally as The Poets Estate.

Westmead Road tram depot, 1919. Trams ran from West Croydon to the tram terminus at the Grapes in Sutton from 1906. The fare for the entire journey was 3 ½ d. In 1935 trolley buses were introduced and remained in use until the depot was used for buses from 1959 to 1964. The building is now used for commercial storage.

Portsmouth Yard, a depository yard used for storage and owned by a Mr Portsmouth, c. 1933. It was situated off Thickett Crescent where Godstone Close stands today.

The Broadway, Lower Road, *c.* 1908. Mr and Mrs J.A. Cruwys extended their confectionery shop into No. 4 The Broadway in 1908 and continued trading here until 1916. Their son Will took this postcard with him, as he travelled on the boat to Freemantle, Western Australia. He gave it to a young man he met on the boat with whom he became 'quite dear old pals' to send home to his family. Although they did not live in Sutton they shared with Will a mutual friend in 'Uncle Harry who lived in The High Street'.

Opposite above: The Broadway, Lower Road, *c.* 1912. Originally the area east of the High Street had meadows either side of Manor Lane up to The Broadway which was where Carshalton lavender fields began. This was a terrace of shops built in the late 1880s for the people of Sutton's growing Newtown district. The area was becoming a thriving community at the time with its own school, a church and nine public houses for the increasing population.

Opposite below: The Broadway, 1912. The shops on the right of this picture situated between Lind Road and Manor Lane form one of the oldest surviving terraces of shops in Sutton. Built in the early 1860s they were known as Alexandra Terrace until 1880. When this photograph was taken the shops included a greengrocer's, fishmonger's, draper's and a coffee tavern.

THE BROADWAY SUTTON.

The Broadway, Sutton.

S & M Series.

Benhill Wood Road, Sutton

Sutton, Benhilton "The Hilton"

Benfleet Hall, Sutton.

Above: Benfleet Hall, Benhill Wood Road, 1918. Built by local builder Mr E. Rabbits in the 1860s, Benfleet Hall was set in extensive grounds in Benhill Wood. In 1890 William Appleton, a tea merchant, became one in a succession of rich and influential residents to own the hall. He lived here with his wife Charlotte and third son Herbert who was an eminent architect of the time. Amongst Herbert's designs in Sutton were the Baptist church in Hill Road, Sutton Public Offices and Sutton County School. He also designed Haselmere in Brighton Road (see p. 65) for his elder brother and family. After William Appleton's death the Holman family rented the hall during which time it was badly damaged by fire, shortly after suffering a serious burglary for which no one was ever arrested even though many of the stolen goods were recovered in London. The hall was restored and became a hospital for injured soldiers during the First World War (see p. 110). After the war Miss H. Gifford rented Benfleet Hall and it became The Marie Souvester School for Girls. In the mid 1930s this lovely old house with such an interesting past was demolished and the many houses between Benhill Wood Road and Benhill Road, including Benfleet Close, stand on the site today.

Opposite above: Benhill Wood Road, c. 1905. In the 1860s this was literally a road through Benhill Wood. It led to exclusive residences such as Benfleet Hall and The Hilton. Although there had been much deforestation since the 1820s, a large triangle of oak trees remained between Benhill Wood Road and All Saints Road until 1900. A few of these old oak trees remain dotted around even today.

Opposite below: The Hilton, Benhill Wood Road, 1904. This was a large house situated where Nos 33A to 39C stand today. Built in the 1870s, it had a string of notable owners including Lieutenant General Sir Michael Kennedy of the Royal Engineers who was Knight Commander of the Royal Star of India. He was a widower living here with his daughters Katherine and Edith who were often left in the company of the three domestic servants whilst their father was away.

Above: Benhill Avenue, 1911. This road was the route for trams running from The Grapes in Sutton to West Croydon. In 1914 routes from Tooting to Belmont were introduced and on Sundays and Bank Holidays two routes – Camden Town to Burgh Heath and Camberwell Green to Kingswood – ran via Sutton. They were however of little use to people of Sutton, being packed with day-trippers from London on their way to picnic in the countryside.

Above: Benhill Street and Union Club, *c.* 1908. This building, now the Conservative Club in Benhill Avenue, was built on the land of Sutton Manor House which consisted of about 13 ½ acres, with large conservatories growing grapes, oranges and pineapples. There were three ornamental ponds and an icehouse. The Manor house itself stood approximately where Kwik Fit stands today. George Orme, the last owner, moved here in the early 1860s with his wife Emma and four young daughters. Emma and baby Agnes died shortly after moving to the Manor House and George remarried, his second wife Jane sadly losing twin girls, Julia and Jane, the day they were born. The estate was originally enclosed by a tree-lined bank, but when cottages were built in Manor Lane and Place, George, who had a reputation for mixing little with the people of Sutton, built a high wall to ensure privacy. Part of this wall still stands today, to the right of the Conservative Club. After Jane's death in 1882, George remained at the Manor House with his daughter Florence until his death in 1895, when the house was demolished and the land sold for the development of a large area east of the High Street, including Litchfield Road and the northern stretches of Lenham and Warwick Road.

Opposite below: Brunswick Road, *c.* 1905, showing a very different view from today. There has been a large amount of development of flats in the road and only one of the large Victorian houses remains. A post box with the Royal crest of Queen Victoria is still set in the gatepost of Brunswick Court. It is a small reminder of the time when the house, then called Advie, was used as a doctor's surgery for Sutton's Victorian residents.

Lewis Road, *c.* 1918. The houses in this road, similar to those that used to stand in Marshall's Road (see p. 36) were the homes of better-off working-class families, such as Samuel Faulkner, a plumber, and his wife Elizabeth, whose son Arthur joined his father in the family business and daughter Agnes became a dressmaker.

Oakhill Road was developed in the late 1860s through Benhill Wood. Although it was much more developed by the time this picture was taken in 1915, it retained a rural atmosphere for many years. There was a brickyard in the area and in Victorian times, with such great demand for bricks, it would have been working to full capacity and the village of Sutton was covered with the smell of burning clay when the wind blew from the north.

Six

North Sutton:
Towards Rosehill

The Green, *c.* 1950.

Bushey Road, 1914. This area was first developed in the 1860s from The Green through Glebelands, with only four houses, until it became the scene above fifty years later. In 1890 an outbreak of scarlet fever in the area caused a temporary hospital to be converted from two cottages at its corner with Collingwood Road. It was decided it should be retained and it was furnished, largely by public donations, to accommodate fourteen patients. It was in use until it was replaced by the hospital in Hill Road in 1902.

The Green, c. 1900. When Sutton Common was enclosed in 1810 The Green was reserved forever as a free recreation ground for the people of Sutton. The large house to the right of this picture was Elmsleigh, formerly called Sorrento Villa, after which the present Sorrento Road is named.

The Green, 1908. The ornate drinking fountain shown here was erected in 1902 to commemorate the coronation of Edward VII. In terracotta green, it must have made an imposing sight raised on its steps. It is sad to realize that these boys relaxing after a game of football would have been fighting in the trenches of France within ten years.

The Green, 1910. Looking down Sorrento Road with Elmsleigh Lodge on the right, the shop at the end, now a veterinary surgery, was E. Pearce's general stores, located at 21 Stayton Road, which was formerly known locally as Mr Murray's meadow.

The Green, 1910. This idyllic view of children playing on a sunny summer's afternoon brings to mind a time when Sutton must have been a much more peaceful town with a slower pace of life. The cows being driven past All Saints' graveyard would probably be on their way to one of the slaughterhouses in the High Street, such as Stevens the butcher's on the corner of Benhill Street.

The Green, Sutton.

The Green in 1910 was overlooked by substantial houses such as The Elms and Rosedale, which still stand today. In the north-east corner of The Green, behind where the postman is standing, a public air-raid shelter was excavated during the Second World War, for people to run to if they were out and about when the air-raid siren sounded. There were many complaints locally about the uncomfortable state of this air-raid shelter and the public one in Collingwood Road recreation ground, which was apparently in a worse state. One woman wrote a letter complaining to Sutton Council saying that even though 150 to 200 people slept in the shelter every night, it was running with water in wet weather and she feared it was unhealthy for her children.

The Victoria Pond, situated on the opposite side of Bushey Road to The Green, had a reputation in the 1890s more for the strength of its smells than its beauty. Following many local complaints it was decided the pond should be cleaned, laid with a firm base and have railings added, hopefully to become an ornament to the district and a place where mothers and children could meet. Obviously the plans were successful as this 1907 picture shows.

The Victoria Pond, 1910. The weeping willow tree on the ornamental island was planted to commemorate Queen Victoria's coronation in 1838. An elm was added on her Diamond Jubilee sixty years later and an oak on the Coronation of Edward VII in 1902. The pond was drained in 1955 and only a slightly raised area in the grass of the present small garden shows where the island once stood.

Angel Bridge, 1935. A lovely landmark of old Sutton was the ornamental bridge built across Angel Hill cutting for pedestrians crossing from Sutton Common Road to All Saints Road. Unfortunately one of the supports cracked and the bridge had to be removed in 1937.

Angel Bridge, c. 1938. This temporary steel girder bridge was built to replace the old ornamental one but it was destroyed by a German bomb during the Second World War, on the night of 10 September 1940, during a week of heavy bombing in Sutton.

Above: Angel Bridge, *c.* 1950. This second temporary bridge was installed to replace the one destroyed by a bomb. It had enough clearance to allow double decker buses to pass safely through. This bridge remained for thirty years when the cutting was rebuilt and the present Angel Bridge built.

Left: Angel Hill, *c.* 1911. The children playing around these magnificent elm trees, which unfortunately have not survived, led a very different life to the children today. Although there was the worry of illness – scarlet fever, diphtheria, measles and tuberculosis were all killers – the children enjoyed much simpler pleasures. A great annual treat at the time was the outing of about 140 Sunday school children, in the company of the Revd Turner and his wife, to Box Hill. The children would set off with their packed lunches in the morning, returning at 8pm. One wonders if today's children would consider a round walk of about twenty-six miles a treat!

The Angel Inn, built around the early part of the nineteenth century, c. 1905. The landlord for many years was John Lynn who lived here with his wife Mary, son and daughter and several lodgers. In the Angel Yard behind the inn, Thomas Jackson kept stables and worked as a horse-breaker. No doubt, as with the Greyhound and Cock Inn, the stagecoaches changed horses here while their passengers took refreshment.

Angel Hill in 1911: this is the original steep hill, through which the cutting was made. The stretch from Rosehill to The Angel was a virtually impassable quagmire for the winter months of the year. The cottages in the picture had steps up to their doors indicating how muddy it once was. The cutting was possibly made in the 1770s to carry heavy rainwater from the stretch outside The Angel to The Green, to drain into the old pond.

The corner of Sutton Common Road, c. 1910. In the 1840s on the land across the common there was only the Plough inn, two large houses, Oldfields Farm and farm cottages, but in the 1860s the road was developed. The district was very attractive, the road well laid with ditches at the sides, and by 1868 twenty-nine large residences, many with cottages for coachmen, had been built for some of Sutton's richest and most influential people.

Sutton Common Road, c. 1910. Although most of the old houses have gone a footpath called Coombe Walk still runs to Hallmead Road by the Green. The name indicates a stream would probably have once run down the hill at this spot. In the early 1800s the path ran through fields passing only one house, the home of George Ferridge, a brickmaker, and his family from around 1825 until his death in 1873 when his eldest son, also called George, a farrier, lived here with his family.

All Saints Road was known in 1908 as Benhill Road from this junction at Angel Hill, curving round to Lower Road and down St Barnabas Road to Carshalton Road. In the present-day recreation ground there was once a large pond and during very cold winters in the 1880s children would skate on the ice, illuminated at night with candles in jam jars.

Woodend Garden Suburb, seen here in around 1920, was designed along the lines of garden suburbs in Hampstead and Ealing. The houses were plotted at not more than nine per acre, giving larger gardens, and all the mature forest trees were preserved. Tenants entered into a co-partnership agreement, paying a deposit of £10 and the rent agreed upon, for which they would receive 4 ½ per cent per annum from profits.

Rosehill in around 1905, looking away from Sutton, with Oldfields Farm on the left. A farm of eighty-one acres was mentioned as far back as 1496, and it was one of the oldest farms in Sutton, lying from Rosehill to The Angel. Sutton's northern tollgate was situated at about the spot where Rosehill roundabout stands today, but after its closure in 1882 the tollhouse was moved to Wrythe Green where it stands today.

Rosehill Roundabout, 1950. The St Helier Estate was built between 1928 and 1936 on 825 acres of farmland previously mainly used for the local lavender and herb industry. 40,000 people, rehoused from the decaying inner London area, were accommodated in 9,000 houses and flats. The community included eighteen schools, seven churches, sixty shops, a 2,000-seater Gaumont cinema and two large pubs, the St Helier Arms and the Rose, pictured here. Both have now been demolished.

Seven

Childhood Days

Sutton Scouts and Cub Scouts, 1970.

Above: Sutton Cub Scouts on a St George's Day parade around 1958 in Grove Road at the junction of Sutton Park Road.

Left: Crown Road School Nativity play, 1962.

Opposite below: Sutton County School library, 1928. In 1920 Manor Park House was used as an annexe for the school, holding the overspill of boys. Then in 1928 the original school and the annexe were replaced by this new building in Manor Lane, which was named Sutton Manor School. It was a large modern building with up-to-date facilities, accommodating 400 pupils. Sutton Grammar School as it is now called is currently preparing for its centenary celebrations.

Above: Sutton County School, Manor Lane, in 1928. The school was originally opened in 1899 by Surrey County Council in Throwley Road, and held 150 boys. In the evenings it was used as a technical institute, holding 300 adult students. Its catchment area covered about fifty square miles and scores of schoolboys would commute daily to Sutton. Sutton County School met a constantly growing demand, by 1915 holding 200 boys instead of the 150 it had been designed to contain.

The Convent from the Lake, Carshalton.

Carshalton House had become St Philomena's School by the time these pictures were taken in 1910. The earliest records of it date back to 1696. The mansion was purchased by Sir John Fellowes in 1716 who transformed the estate. He built the high brick wall, which encloses it today, and the wrought iron gates in Pound Street. Sir John was a director of the South Sea Company, which collapsed in 1721, leading to his imprisonment in the Tower of London for a short time.

The Water Tower was one of the luxurious additions Sir John Fellowes made to supply water to Carshalton House. Other features were the Hermitage, an ornamental lake and stables. Sir John never married and after his death in 1724 aged fifty-four, he left Carshalton House to his brother Edward. He also generously left money to his friends, family and to all his servants. Particularly mentioned was £100 to 'Charles Caesar, my Indian boy, who may be destitute when I am gone'.

St Philomena's senior girls' sitting room, *c.* 1910. The Daughters of The Cross bought Carshalton House in 1893 after it had lain empty for a decade. Before this it had been used as a cadet school for the Royal Artillery and Engineers and for twenty-four years it had been a private boys' school. The first girl borders arrived on 31 August 1893 and St Philomena's Convent was born.

St Philomena's dressmaking class, *c.* 1910. The school quickly won a high reputation in this country and abroad. Many of the girls had English parents working overseas. As well as the usual school subjects, first aid, home nursing, cookery and dressmaking were taught and a heated swimming bath was built in 1909. By 1910 three tennis courts had been laid out and by 1921 the playing fields covered an acre and a half.

Sutton High School For Girls, c. 1905. In 1881 Edward Solly put Park House, Cheam Road, up for sale. It had five bedrooms, a library with 30,000 books, a boot room and butler's room and extensive gardens with a coach house and croquet lawn. In 1883 it was leased to the Girls' Public Day School Company, initially for twenty-one years. On 17 January 1884, with eight teachers and Miss Whyte as headmistress, Park House was opened to eighty girls.

The gymnasium at Sutton High School for Girls, c. 1910. This had been outgrown by the time the school celebrated its golden jubilee in 1934 and the building of a new one was commenced, which was opened in 1935. In 1911 the school was enlarged when the trust leased Fernwood, a private house, which stood where the Holiday Inn car park is today, for use as a junior department until 1932. In that year The Homestead and Suffolk House, which adjoined Park House, were purchased and became the Kindergarten and Juniors building respectively.

Sutton High School for Boys, Cheam Road, opened in 1879 and accepted boys of five to eighteen years of age. It prepared them for either taking their Common Entrance exams at thirteen or for staying on and taking their Matriculation examination. The curriculum included Classics, mathematics, physics, chemistry and English, with provision for games and boxing. This picture dates from 1911 and the school finally closed in 1961.

Benhilton College and Kindergarten at Nos 1 and 2 Burnell Road, c. 1905. Advertised in 1898 as a school for the daughters of gentlemen, by the time this photograph was taken a small number of boys had obviously been accepted. The children were instructed in English language and literature, French, German, drawing and singing. Champion Timber Merchants stands on the site of the school today.

South Metropolitan District School, c. 1900. In the 1840s in London alone there were at least 30,000 destitute children outside the workhouse. Either orphans or abandoned by their parents, the children begged and many turned to crime. Around 1850 schools known as industrial schools were built in Great Britain to try to house these children. This school, built in 1853, housed between 1,400 and 1,500 pauper children from five London parishes and was situated in Brighton Road on the far side of the valley known as Crown Bottom where the houses of Belmont Heights stand today.

Fire at the South Metropolitan District School. On 13 November 1856, in the early hours of the morning, fire broke out in a blanket store of the new south wing, occupied by the girls. Because of the lack of water and the large amount of timber, the fire quickly spread. Luckily no one was killed or injured but hundreds of children were left sitting on the grass, crying and holding the little ones. Mr Overton, a local farmer, kindly took the younger children and the sick into his nearby farmhouse and buildings, until their return the following day to the remaining north wing.

South Metropolitan District School, 1872. By 1857 it was decided that any vagrant children, even if they had committed no offence, should be sent to an Industrial School. The children were taught trades such as engineering, tailoring (shown in this picture of a classroom from the *London Illustrated News*), shoemaking or carpentry and large numbers of the boys and girls were sent out every year to service or apprenticeship. The elder boys farmed on a homestead of 50-60 acres and learned to play musical instruments, often going on to careers in military bands. With playrooms and a large swimming bath the description sounds comfortable, but it must be remembered that life was very hard for children who lived there at the time. The school had a high death rate mainly because the children were young and undernourished. In 1876 alone twenty-two children died in a matter of weeks when there was an epidemic of measles in Sutton. The school was known as 'Linger and Die' by Sutton's inhabitants for this reason. Around the end of the nineteenth and the beginning of the twentieth centuries some rethinking was being done as to better alternatives for orphan children, such as foster families and this school closed in 1902. The building had many uses after this, including a camp for German prisoners of war in the First World War and an emergency hospital for victims of the Blitz in London in the Second World War. Between the wars it was used as a workhouse but for many years, until it closed in 1982, the building was used as a psychiatric hospital and an industrial neurosis unit. A further fire finally caused its destruction, ending the life of a building with such a full history.

Eversfield, Mulgrave Road, started life as a private girls' day and boarding school in Cheam Road at the beginning of the twentieth century. It was situated on the corner of Western Road. In 1933 Eversfield School moved into the building shown here, which prior to this had been used as a private hotel called Ravens Court.

Eversfield library, c. 1935. An advertisement for the school in 1938 stated that the aim was to give a healthy and happy school life and prepare the girls for London Matriculation examinations or university entrance examinations, as well as giving careful supervision to matters of health, manners and habits of neatness. Eversfield closed during the Second World War but the building still stands as an old peoples' residential home. The name Eversfield has been preserved.

West Street National School, *c.* 1880. In 1852 a piece of land on Sutton Downs was sold and the money was used to build this school, which replaced two charity schools in the village. Mr Gosling, owner of the Manor House at the time, donated the site and Mr Alcock, Lord of the Manor, made a generous contribution towards its building cost. It was supported by St Nicholas' church and financial donations from wealthy local residents. The school closed in 1968 and was finally demolished in 1971.

Gym class at Robin Hood Junior School, Thorncroft Road, *c.* 1972.

New Town School, c. 1915. A school board for Sutton was formed in April 1874. West Street school was transferred to the Board and a school was built in Greyhound Road for the children in the growing Newtown district. It was opened on 28 June 1876 and consisted of an infants' school in the centre and a boys' and girls' classroom on either side. There were lobbies to each room with 'Macfarlane's Patent Lavatories' and large playgrounds at the rear fitted with earth closets. National School children in the 1870s paid a fee each Monday of one penny for the infants and twopence for seniors. The school was extended in the 1920s and has since become Manor Park Primary School.

Eight

The War Years

Benfleet Hall War Hospital, 1918.

Benfleet Hall, Sutton.

HAIG WARD,
BENFLEET HALL WAR HOSPITAL, SUTTON.

S. & W. Series.

KITCHENER WARD,
BENFLEET HALL WAR HOSPITAL, SUTTON
S. & W. SERIES.

Above: Kitchener Ward, 1918. The men in this picture must have been relieved to receive a 'Blighty' – a wound serious enough to send them home. They enjoyed excellent care, many visiting long after being discharged. A stark contrast was the fate of one nineteen-year-old Sutton man who was wounded at the Battle of Cambrai on 30 November 1917 and captured by the Germans. Rifleman Frank Brown of the 18th Battalion London Regiment, well known and liked in the area, wrote to his parents in Cressingham Grove, Sutton on the 28 December 1917 saying, 'They have just extracted the bullets from my legs. I hope to be up and about in eight to ten weeks.' However, despite numerous letters and parcels sent to him, nothing more was heard of Frank until September 1918, when notification came from the War Office that Rifleman Frank E. Brown had died on 1 January 1918 of wounds received in action.

Opposite above: Benfleet Hall War Hospital, 1918. To assist with the many wounded servicemen returned to England during the First World War, large houses such as Benfleet Hall in Benhill Wood Road were converted to hospitals. This was opened on the 11 June 1915, with sixty beds, for use as a Red Cross Hospital, under the care of Dr Hooper. The hospital was entirely funded by donations from local people, who gave money so generously, that it was soon able to accommodate seventy-two patients.

Opposite below: Haig Ward, 1918. The servicemen convalesced in Benfleet Hall's comfortable surroundings, in summer enjoying the extensive grounds by relaxing in deckchairs or playing croquet and bowls. The less physically fit spent time playing games such as draughts, chess and dominoes. The hospital was run by two matrons who worked with a small team of trained nurses, but a large number of Sutton girls gave their services as voluntary aid workers for the duration of the war.

Sutton County School swimming team, 1914. Sydney Neville Levitt (seated behind the cup) was born on 6 November 1898, and lived with his family in Mulgrave Road, Sutton. In 1911 he was awarded a scholarship to Sutton County School, where he excelled, being captain of the cricket, football and swimming teams. He was a leading member of the debating society and enjoyed writing poetry.

Sutton County School prefects, 1914. After leaving school in 1916, Sydney (second from left, front row), was posted to the Army Training Reserve in 1917. He was granted a commission in the Kings Royal Rifle Corps and by Easter 1918 was in France. On 29 September 1918 at 5.30am he was with the 16th Battalion, who were assembled in a trench on the crest of a hill awaiting an attack on the village of Ossus in Northern France.

During the attack, the enemy put down a thick gas barrage and the company became separated in the confusion and the fog. Finding themselves surrounded, 2nd Lieutenant Sydney Levitt took a small party to try and find a way through. They did not return and his body was found next day, close to enemy lines. He is buried here in Northern France with the other members of his battalion who lost their lives that day.

In a poem found after he was killed, Sydney tragically prophesied his death:

Abschied Vom Leben
The wound burns hot; my quivering lips are pale,
My heart is nigh to burst beneath the strain,
Now I await the end of Life's short reign,
And breathe 'Thy will be done'. Nought can avail,
For now the shadows of Death do e'en assail
Mine eyes, where golden peace had once domain.

Yet courage, heart! The fond ideals we gain
On earth must live with us beyond Death's pale,
And what I held as sacred here below,
That which set youthful ardour all aglow,
The pride of freedom and the charm of love,
I see their forms seraphic up above,
And as my body sinks down into Night,
They bear my spirit upwards to the Light.

The War Memorial, Manor Park, was dedicated at this ceremony in 1921 to the 519 men and one woman from Sutton who lost their lives during the Great War. The one woman whose name appears is Eliza Bailey, aged twenty-two, who was one of the five remembered that were killed in accidents at the munitions factory based at Brocks firework factory in Gander Green Lane.

Right: Private Charles Ford in 1944. He grew up living on the St Helier Estate, first in Robertsbridge Road then Simms Close. After leaving school, Charles started working in a men's outfitters in Sutton High Street before being called up and joining the 5th Dorset Regiment. He was sent to France in 1944 and joined the Allied forces advancing through Germany in April 1945.

Below: In order to delay the advancing Allied forces, the Germans, who were retreating rapidly, placed sea-mines under the road. This poignant photograph shows Private Charles Ford, then aged nineteen, and A Company 5th Dorset Regiment on Sunday 29 April 1945 in a kangaroo tank, minutes before it was blown up on a mine and the entire section, including Charles, lost their lives. Less than a week later on 5 May the ceasefire was declared.

Left: Sergeant Cecil Murdoch, Royal Signals Corps, on leave with his wife Elsie in Manor Park in 1940. Before this, in May 1940, Cecil was one of approximately 224,000 men of the British forces evacuated in a flotilla of British ships, both large and small, from Dunkirk. After having made the journey in a coal barge from near Dunkirk, Cecil arrived in Weymouth covered in coal dust, but able to send Elsie a postcard at their home in Thickett Crescent, Sutton, saying he was safe in the place they spent their third holiday together. This coded message passed the censors, but told Elsie he was safely home in England.

Below: Thickett Crescent, 1940. Daphne Murdoch must have been very proud of this smart doll's pram she is seen here playing with outside her house, which shows the criss-cross tape on the windows to help protect against injury if the glass was shattered. During the Blitz, 337 bombs were dropped on the Borough of Sutton from 30 August 1940 until 28 July 1941 alone, causing great destruction and loss of life.

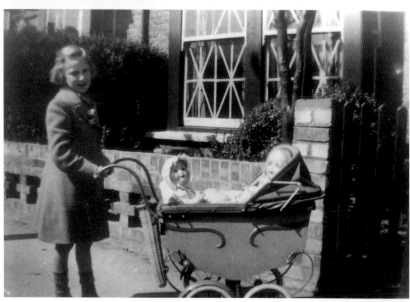

A children's party in Simms Close in May 1945. Many of these children would have no other memories than those of life at war. Despite this, Joan Ford, who lived here, has only memories of a happy childhood. Her father kept chickens and rabbits and grew vegetables so the family did not suffer food shortages, although Joan does remember missing sweets as her ration for the week was only ¼ lb! Children would take with them to school packed lunches and barley sugars in case there was an air raid during the school day and they had to go down into the shelters.

VE Day celebrations in Simms Close, St Helier, May 1945. It must have been with very mixed feelings that some of the residents of Simms Close celebrated their VE Day street party. Behind the smiles of this close-knit community, great tragedies had been suffered. The houses were bombed twice; in one incident when the houses suffered a direct hit a young boy was killed. It is still possible to see the repairs in the roofs after the bomb damage. Mrs Goulding (front right) lost her twenty-four-year-old son Leslie at Arnhem and Mrs Ford's (front left) son Charlie was killed in Germany just two weeks before this photograph was taken.

VE Day celebrations, Thickett Crescent, May 1945. Scenes like this were repeated all over the borough in this month. Beautifully decorated and often floodlit streets were the venues for parties, which continued late into the night. Food rationing was still at its height but great ingenuity was shown in times of extreme shortage. Typical were Dibdin Road and Dibdin Close whose residents held a combined party with film shows, a bonfire, fireworks and pony rides. In Sydney Road children gave a concert for their parents and friends, collecting money for the Great Ormond Street Children's Hospital. The adults worked wonders producing magnificent spreads of food for the children including jelly, blancmange and ice cream.

Nine

One Sutton Family: The Bawtrees

Brambleacres, c. 1900. Samuel Bawtree was born in 1830 and became an apprentice in the Merchant Navy during the war between the United States and Mexico in 1845. After becoming a Lloyds underwriter he married Phoebe Wells in June 1856, moving to Sutton in 1867. They lived in Elmwood, Cheam Road; Samuel bought the land for Brambleacres in that year. The house was completed in 1871 and Samuel and Phoebe moved in with their eight children and three servants.

Left: Brambleacres was a twenty-roomed house set in two and a half acres of grounds on the southern side of Worcester Road. The entire top floor was used as a vast playroom for the Bawtree children, Arthur, Edith, May, Harold, Percy, Bernard, Winifred and Christine whose ages ranged from thirteen years to nine months when they moved into the house. Two iron rings were screwed into the attic room's ceiling and a swing was attached to them for the children to play on.

Below: Percy was the only one of Samuel and Phoebe's children to marry. He married Margaret Anderson of Hazeldene, Cheam Road, Sutton, on 27 June 1900 at the Congregational church. The couple spent their married life in Wallington until their retirement in 1936, when they moved to Cheam. They had six sons; tragically two died as a result of the Second World War. This picture shows (left to right) Phoebe, Harold, Christine, Percy and Margaret, Viola and William and Anne Anderson, brother and mother of the bride.

Percy and Margaret Bawtree in 1935. The Bawtree family lived in Sutton for over 100 years. They were liked and respected and have left their mark in many ways in the area.

Above: Brambleacres garden, *c.* 1915. Percy and Margaret's six sons, two of whom are pictured here, would often visit their aunts and uncles. When the three eldest boys, Donald, Stewart and Arthur, were quarantined with mumps they stayed at Brambleacres and Aunt Christine would take them for long walks on Banstead Downs, keeping them entertained with stories. These days were fondly remembered by the boys as the 'mump walks'.

Left: Arthur Wells Bawtree, *c.* 1900. Arthur was the eldest of Samuel and Phoebe's children and started the Cadet Corps at St Barnabas' church. Harold was the most athletic member of the family, playing rugger for an amateur Sutton team; Percy was for some time a member of Sutton Urban Council; and Bernard was a shy, generous man giving money anonymously to local good causes, including funding the Parish Hall at Belmont. The four sisters were all kind charitable ladies who gave their time to many good causes including Broadstairs Children's Home which Christine in particular supported, taking great pleasure in making beautifully wrapped Christmas presents for the children.

Brambleacres garden, c. 1900. In 1951, Christine, the only surviving member of the Bawtree children, whose dearest wish was that Brambleacres should not fall to the developer, generously presented the house and adjoining field to the Borough of Sutton for use as an old people's home. After Christine's death a modern residential home was built on the field and the family name lives on in Bawtree House. Sadly though, despite Christine's hopes, Brambleacres was demolished in 1991 and the houses of Brambleacres Close stand on the site today.

Durlstone, Mulgrave Road, c. 1880. Alfred Bawtree, Samuel's younger brother, and Matilda Clark married in 1873 and moved to Sutton in 1874. After several years living in Manor Lane then Lenham Road they moved to this house with their three children, Alfred, Sylvia and Athelstone. Young Alfred is pictured here by the gate. During the ten years they lived here they had two more daughters, Viola and Elaine. Durlstone still stands at number 100, Mulgrave Road.

Blackwater House (seen here *c.* 1890) stood at the end of George Street where the UCI cinema stands today and was home of the Bawtree family for ten years, their youngest son Ivan being born here in 1894. One of Ivan's early memories was of looking down into the fields behind the house at the gypsy caravans and roundabouts of visiting fairs. He remembered lying in bed watching the lights twirling on his ceiling and listening to the music of popular songs of the time.

Clapham Lodge, *c.* 1900. Built in 1864 for Miss Lucy Thornton, a member of the wealthy 'Clapham set', Clapham Lodge was set in two acres of gardens in the middle of farmland near Banstead Downs and was home to the Bawtree family from 1900 onwards. Until the early 1930s there was no gas, electricity or mains water supplied to the house. Lighting was by candles and oil lamps and water from a pump by the cellar door.

Right: Alfred and Matilda Bawtree in 1900. Alfred, a Lloyds underwriter, was born the youngest of ten children in Stoke Newington, North London, in 1846 and Matilda was born near Orpington, Kent, in 1849. After moving to Sutton both were deeply involved in the Congregational church in Carshalton Road. Alfred was a deacon, church secretary and Sunday school superintendent and Matilda took women's Bible classes on Sunday afternoons. Sadly, after losing his sight in 1913 Alfred had to resign his church duties but continued to walk the two miles to attend services with Elaine.

Below: Viola Bawtree at Clapham Lodge Gate, *c.* 1900. Clapham Lodge was situated on a farm track called Carshalton Lane, now Banstead Road South, two miles from Sutton town. Matilda would make the weekly trip in a pony and trap but others would walk across fields from the back garden, which came out under a barbed wire fence in Langley Park Road opposite Egmont Road. The house, surrounded by fields, was so isolated that on foggy days a brass bell was rung to guide any family member walking home.

Sylvia (sitting) and Viola Bawtree in 1902. They were both charitable ladies giving their services to many local causes. Viola, an artistic, romantic young woman, was deaf after suffering scarlet fever as a child. Although never going out to work and being very retiring Viola was passionate about gardening and the garden diaries she wrote for many years showed great sensitivity towards other people and a wonderful sense of humour. After nursing Elaine before she died, Sylvia died of a heart attack in 1950. Viola lived into her ninetieth year, looking after her beloved garden for almost seventy years.

Alfred Bawtree, the eldest son of Alfred and Matilda, 1900. He was an inventor who found fame but not fortune, being the first man to produce a record of sound on film which could be played back, long before talking pictures. He married Lucy Legg in 1902 and lived at Lynton Manor Park Road, now No. 20. Sadly, like his father, he lost his sight in the last twelve years of his life. His younger brother Athelstone started a printing and developing business in the attic of Lynton before moving to his shop in Station Approach, well known for many years in Sutton. Athelstone started the Boys' Brigade at Belmont free church and married Daisy, adopting one daughter called Shirley.

Clapham Lodge drawing room in 1900 – it was used as a best room for special occasions. The door had panels painted with daffodils and a glass fronted cupboard in the corner of the room was full of miniatures collected by Sylvia, Viola and Elaine during the 'Grand Tour'. On either side of the fireplace hung an Electrophone, which was a pre-radio system of listening to concerts from places such as the Albert Hall and Crystal Palace over telephone wires.

Ivan Bawtree in the garden of Clapham Lodge, c. 1900. After attending Sutton County School, Ivan served as a corporal in the Royal Engineers during the First World War, photographing 2,870 war graves for the Red Cross. He trained as a photographic engraver and worked for Kodak for thirty years, also enjoying photography as a hobby; moreover he was a keen gardener. A captain in the Belmont Boys' Life Brigade, Ivan received a gold watch in 1956 for fifty years' service. After receiving an MBE in 1977, Ivan, the sole survivor of the Bawtree children, died at Clapham Lodge in 1979, the house he had lived in almost all his life.

Viola Bawtree, 1900. After Viola's death in 1973 Ivan, sadly, had to sell Clapham Lodge's gardens to pay death duties. The houses of Bawtree Close stand on the gardens today and after being badly damaged by fire in 1988 it seemed the house would also come to a sad end. Fortunately Clapham Lodge, a Grade II listed building, has been bought and restored. Although the large gardens have gone, many of the mature trees remain in the close, including the Friendship Tree, a copper beech named by a romantic young Viola nearly a hundred years ago.

Acknowledgements

Grateful thanks are due to the following people who supplied information, allowed access to archive material and gave permission for reproduction of photographs:
The staff at Sutton Central Library - especially the staff in the Archive and Local Studies Searchroom; the staff at the Public Records Office, Kew; the staff at Sutton Cemetery; Mr Harold Bawtree; Major (Retd) R.D. Cassidy MBE, Curator of the Royal Green Jackets Museum; Mr and Mrs Gasparelli; Mrs Joan Gore (née Ford); Mr Russell Gore, War Research Society; Mr G. Ironside, Headmaster of Sutton Grammar School; Mrs Anne Knee; Miss Daphne Murdoch; Mr Ken Rogers MBE and Mrs Sheila Rogers; Mrs Joyce Roseberg (née Bawtree); Mrs Susan Ruck; Mrs Jean Smith.